THE WRECK OF TH

AT POLDHU CC

The tragic loss of the dutch barque "Jonkheer Meester van de Wall van Putterschoek". Only one survivor was left alive to tell the story.

Robert Felce BSc (Hons)

First Edition 2015

Published by Robert Felce BSc (Hons)

ISBN 978-0-9569895-2-9

Printed by Westcountry Printing and Publishing

Churchtown, Mullion, Helston TR127HQ

Acknowledgements

I would like to thank Jean M.A. van Wageningen in Dordrecht for his help and interest in allowing new information to become an integral part of the story.
I wish to thank Shane Griffiths, Vicar of Mullion, for helping to add impetus to the research. Coincidence is often an unexplainable thing.
Finally, a special thanks to the Joodlebug, for helping me to decide whether this story might actually make sense to the reader.

Cover Photo; "Mullion Roads- helpless on the lee shore" by author, 2011

Contents

Introduction

This story is not just about a shipwreck.

The *Jonkheer*, sailed the world for nearly two years and was returning home to Rotterdam on the last stage of a long journey. Almost within sight of home and in a storm she became embayed in the Mounts Bay, off the Lizard Peninsula. The winter of 1867 was a winter of storms, shipwrecks and flooding in Cornwall. As usual, the coast of the Lizard Peninsula near to Mullion sheltered hundreds of sailing ships, unable to negotiate the most southerly point of England, and had no choice but to take shelter. On a dark March night in 1867 her luck ran out and she struck the Men-y-Grib rocks just south of Poldhu Cove. Twenty Four lives were lost, but there was one survivor, a Greek sailor who spoke no English. The story of the wreck and how it affected Mullion began on the other side of the world.

The Ship

On 25th July 1865 a three masted Dutch Barque named the *Jonkheer Meester van de Wall van Putterschoek,* captained by Klaas Folkerts Lammerts set sail from Helleveotsluis, an outer port of Rotterdam, in the Dutch Province of South Holland, bound for Batavia, Java. She sailed to St. Helena, a regular mid- Atlantic restocking point where inbound and outbound Dutch trading vessels met, and from there on to Buenos Aires, and Montevideo. She then sailed east and with a following wind, on to SW Australia and north to Java, part of the great Dutch sea trading empire.
During an extended trip lasting over a year she visited a number of other SE Asian Trading Ports including Samarang-Billiton (Belitung Island) -Batavia-Melbourne-Newcastle (New South Wales) and Cheribon (Cirebon).
 The *Jonkheer* was a 650 ton register, 1000 tons burthen or load carrying ability, built in 1856 for J. van Wageningen in the Merwede shipyard at Dordrecht.
On 24th November 1866 she left Samarang and Batavia on the return trip to Rotterdam, with her Dutch captain, crew (which included First Mate, Second Mate and Bosun), and 6 passengers who included 3 ladies, one of whom was about 25 years old, and was also expecting a baby. She was believed to be known to the Captain.

The barque was 135` (41m) long and 32` (9m) wide, with a keel of oak, a sleek and fast sailing ship which had made several similar long journeys lasting up to 2 years- an age to be thousands of miles away from home and family (32).

On this trip the *Jonkheer* carried a general cargo of coffee, sugar, arrowroot, spices, and a large quantity of valuable Banka Tin Ingots as ballast, a total reported cargo weight of 850 tons. In 1813 Banka in Indonesia, was producing half as much Tin as the whole of Cornwall (6a). (See appendix). The total value of the cargo was estimated to be between £40,000- £50,000. The cargo would likely have been paid for using a Dutch system called *partenrederij* (partners in the shipping company). Anyone could invest in a fraction of the ship and gain or lose money accordingly. A shipbuilder, a family, the Vicar, the butcher or shoemaker in a community could have invested money in a ship and cargo. The largest investor or accountant was called the *boekhouder* who took the greatest risk (33).

One of the men joining the crew at Batavia was a Greek sailor named Georgio Buffani. He spoke a mixture of Greek, Italian and very little English, a fact that was to become important at the end of this last fateful journey which ended at Poldhu, Cornwall in March the following year. That journey took the ship several thousand nautical miles SSW across the Indian Ocean, around the Cape of Good Hope and into the South Atlantic for the last time. Crossing the equator on a trade route which had been used for hundreds of years she headed north. After leaving Batavia two of the crew became seriously ill and died off the coast of Africa. On the 19th January 1867 the 2 bodies and a third sick crew man were put ashore at the volcanic island of St. Helena in the south Atlantic. Despite its remoteness St. Helena was a regular stopping off point for ships returning from China and the East Indies to replenish water and supplies, and exchange information.

One of the female passengers here took the opportunity to write a letter to her sister living in Manchester before the *Jonkheer* again put to sea. The passenger, Mrs Sophia Woollett was born of English parents in Holland, she went to India and Java and was returning with a large amount of property to her sister Charlotte Schroeder in Manchester, before going on to live in Holland. She had lived in Jakarta in a village or town near Oreanger Regentschaper.
The rest of the journey was not without incident.
Three weeks before arriving off Cornwall the female passenger, believed to be French, gave birth on board to a daughter and 10 days before arriving off the Lizard, one of the crew, Georgio Buffani broke his right arm in an accident aboard ship. There was little by way of medical care.

The Cornish Coast

Early Newspaper reports of the incident indicate that by Saturday 23rd March 1867 she was approaching the Cornish Coast and was not far from the port of Falmouth. Buffani later suggested that he thought that the ship could have put in there. The weather was poor, as it had been all that month, and indeed all that winter. In early January there had been several major storms and shipwrecks in the Mounts Bay, with many lives lost.

By 6am Monday 25th March the *Jonkheer* had made the Lizard, the wind was strong SSW, but she soon became embayed in Mounts Bay. All day the crew made many attempts to tack out of the Bay but failed, yet Captain and crew - now three short, plus a man injured, must have felt confident of their ability to avoid running aground in such an isolated locality, and sail the remaining 460 nautical miles from the Lizard and home to Rotterdam. Again, early newspaper reports of the incident in the Royal Cornwall Gazette indicated that the *Jonkheer* was seen by Mousehole Pilots and the Prussia Cove Coastguard from across the Bay to have become embayed but she continued to try and manoeuvre. The storm continued to worsen and about 3am Tuesday 26th March 1867 during the gale the ship ran aground on the Men-y-Grib rocks between the two sandy coves of Polurrian and Poldhu, driven in by strong winds, losing her masts and breaking in two.

The two sections of the ship were washed north towards Poldhu before sinking back into deeper water, however, three of the crew had managed to cling for life to the jib boom, or extended bowsprit (See Fig.2). As the bow hit the cliffs two were washed away and drowned. One man managed to cling to the rocks until the tide began to recede. He was the only survivor and despite a broken arm remained conscious. Part of the stern section was finally driven onshore at Poldhu but the ship however was broken into many pieces.

The land bordering this part of the coast was unlit and with no lights to help, this terrifying wreck took place in a storm and almost total darkness. The nearest village was Mullion over 1 mile (1.66Km) away to the SE, and not within sight of the sea. The small village of Cury was a similar distance to the NE as was Gunwalloe to the North. The only inhabitants nearby were the sleeping occupants of farms and there were no buildings on the cliff top. Only a small number of coastguards were responsible for the many miles of Lizard coastline which they had to patrol on foot. At night they had to raise the alarm in Mullion, and obtain as much assistance as was possible in a short time (See Fig.3).

The Vicar of Mullion in 1867 was Rev. Edmund George Harvey, an educated man who lived with his Welsh wife Sarah and 5 children at Vicarage House. He was a skilful writer, artist, musician and family man who in

1850 took a B.A. degree at Queens College Cambridge. Afterwards he lived and worked for a few years in Germany. Between 1860 & 1865 he lived in Truro before taking up a position in Mullion Parish.

Whilst he was living and working in Mullion, Rev. Harvey quickly became aware of the difficult situation which existed with the number of shipwrecks and in particular the loss of life in the locality. It caused the local community great concern. Mullion has a history of wrecks stretching back for centuries and the coast also had a historic reputation for the *dismantling and removal of ships and cargo from wreck sites*, as well as for smuggling. Some local properties are believed still to have ships furniture and timbers from shipwrecks in their construction, and there was a time when almost everyone in the locality was involved in *"Free Trading"* with France, mainly for Brandy.

By 1867 this was mostly in the past and now there was a greater degree of vigilance for the safety of ships and seafarers and less emphasis on smuggling. A multitude of sailing ships of the 1800s, sailing to and from all parts of the world, travelled along the Cornish coast, often finding difficulty in rounding the Lizard before making for the English Channel, bound for British and European ports. Depending on wind, weather and tides they often had to anchor and seek shelter off Mullion in the "Mullion Roads" between the Island and Pedngwynian, a mile to the north until weather conditions improved.

An easterly wind, for example, was one which could last for 2-3 weeks, a huge problem for boats anchored in the lee of the cliffs because when the wind changed an anchored sailing ship facing west might find itself quickly being driven onto the cliffs and beaches or into anchor ropes of other ships, with little chance of reaching safety.

Likewise, a ship caught in a W or SW gale and drawn into the Mounts Bay may be able to make headway out of the Bay by "tacking" but sailing ships might often "miss stays", meaning "to make no headway when zig-zagging towards the wind", and ultimately be driven onto the cliffs with fatal consequences.

Even on large vessels, navigation was only fully understood by a limited few and experienced sailors could be hard to find. Full Admiralty and Trade enquiries were often required into the damaging or sinking of a ship with evidence heard and reported in full so that lessons could be learnt- but a very high price was often paid in terms of lives lost.

The sea lanes were yesterday`s motorways and from the 1830s, there were calls for a Harbour of Refuge in the Mounts Bay at Penzance (7). In 1859 there was a call for a Lifeboat to be stationed at Mullion, and in 1868 plans were proposed for a harbour in the Cove and a breakwater to be built offshore between the Island and the mainland at the Vro, because of the high volume of ships requiring shelter in the Mullion Roads at the time.

A letter to the editor of the Royal Cornwall Gazette of 1859 recalled that *"The Lizard is well known to be the highway of the commerce of the world, it has many miles of dangerous coast, and every night there is a risk of collision, yet there is not a Lifeboat on this coast."*

Rev. Harvey wrote on March 15th 1867 that *there had recently been between 400-500 vessels anchoring in the Mullion* Roads. They all got *away safely*, but two barques were in a very critical position for some hours. Had it come on to blow there would have been no chance of escape (3).

Following ferocious storms, several wrecks, and loss of life corresponding with high tides in early January 1867, a Public Meeting was held at Mullion on 14th January calling for a Lifeboat to be introduced in the Cove. It was a call supported by many prominent people in the Parish. After generous financial support was obtained from Lord Robartes at Lanhydrock, and donations received from Methodist organisations, the first Lifeboat, the *Daniel J. Draper* was introduced in September 1867. Harvey became the first Hon. Secretary of Mullion Lifeboat Association and remained so until 1884 (3).

The Report of the wreck

Residents of the village of Mullion know that the sounds of the sea often travel eerily from the coast to the village a mile away and on many a night, the waves can often be heard crashing and booming onto the cliffs and sandy beaches of Mullion and Polurrian.

About 11pm on the evening of 25th March 1867, Rev. Harvey wrote that he was at his home at the vicarage after his family had gone to bed, reading. He could hear the storm outside, but as he listened he thought he could hear the sound of a long shrieking wail and many voices on the storm. Opening the window he listened to the gale outside sweeping in from the sea and the sound of thundering surf on the nearby shore, but he could discern no sound, rocket, or blue light signal of distress, so he went to bed. It was high tide (1. p68).

About 3am the following morning, 26th March 1867 a Coastguard on watch overnight hurried to the village to warn that he had seen a large barque dangerously near to the cliffs and it may have gone ashore. There was no lifeboat at this time and the only alternative for a rescue was the rocket apparatus, which was taken down to the beach at Poldhu. This was a method of firing a rocket with a line attached onto a ship in distress from a cliff top or a beach. A hawser was then hauled out and tied onto the ship and a cradle or bosuns chair was used to rescue crew and passengers. It required 20 or more men to operate it from shore and was limited by the length of the hawser- but on this coast it saved many lives, in particular when a Lifeboat could not be launched (3).

A search was made as far as Gunwalloe, with no success. However, from the cliff tops between Polurrian and Poldhu parts of a wreck became visible. The ship had broken in two. A further search among the rocks at Poldhu revealed an injured man, the Greek Sailor Georgio Buffani- the only survivor.

Buffani was distressed, largely unintelligible and was able to speak only poor English, so little information could be obtained at that time. He seemed to speak in a mixture of Greek and Italian. He was taken to a Coastguard Cottage in Mullion village to be looked after and given clothes. As the tide receded, the bodies of two women wearing only remnants of night clothes were found close to the wreck. A third female body was later found, along with those of a sailor and an infant. It was not uncommon that bodies were washed ashore unclothed, torn off by the currents and the rocks. As was customary at that time the bodies were conveyed to Mullion where they were lodged in the Church Tower to await a Coroner's inquest (See Fig 7)

Prior to 1808 unclaimed bodies delivered ashore by the sea could not be interred in consecrated ground. They were usually buried, often unmarked, on the cliffs or in the valleys close to where they were found, and occasionally, even today, unidentified skeletons have become exposed. Parish records show that between 1808 and 1874 a total of 132 bodies were washed ashore and 67 were buried in Mullion Churchyard.

It was two local shipwrecks on this same Lizard coast which heralded a change in the Law. In November 1807, the sinking of the "*James and Rebecca*" at Halzephron Cliffs and in December 1807 the Royal Navy Frigate "*Anson*" at Loe Bar, led to dreadful loss of life with many bodies remaining unburied for some time. A proposal was drafted by Helston solicitor Thomas Grylls and led to the *Dead Bodies Internment Bill* being introduced by John Tremayne MP, later called the *Burial of Drowned Persons Act 1808* (6b). It provided a 5 shilling (25p) reward for the finding of a corpse and a £5 fine for not disclosing a finding. A further one shilling and sixpence (7½p) was provided to the finder who took the body to the Church plus beer money if the body was decomposing. It allowed provision for decent burials of unidentified remains and unclaimed bodies within the Parish where they were found, bringing the closer association with the Church (2). In the wreck of the *Jonkheer* all bar one body recovered was buried at Mullion. The other recovered body was reportedly buried at Gunwalloe Churchyard. Rev Harvey visited the sole survivor at the cottage but found it difficult to obtain any information. This was mostly due to the language difficulty. It seemed that there had been 25 people aboard at the time and when the vessel struck all of them had been on deck (2). He noted that for a simple sailor Buffani had in his possession a ladies gold watch and chain and he was a little suspicious of the man (1).

15.

Fig 1.below; An original picture of the Jonkheer in full sail. (Courtesy of
blockland.dordtenazoeker.nl)

Fig.2.below photograph; A similar Dutch barque *Euterpe*, built in 1862 at
Dordrecht for J. Van Wageningen. It shows the long bowsprit used to climb to
safety from the *Jonkheer* (Courtesy of blockland.dordtenazoeker.nl)

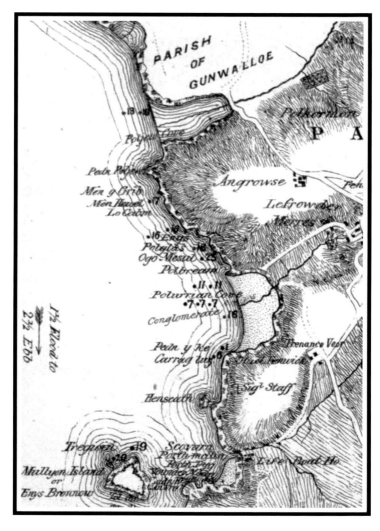

Fig.3 Section of map produced by Lakes of Truro Published in "*Mullion, its history scenery and antiquities...*" by Rev. E.G.Harvey 1875

Fig.4 below; The imposing cliffs at Pedn Poldhu. (Photo by author 2009)

Fig 5 below; The Old Inn, Mullion. Also the 19[th]Century Coroners Court. The Church Tower is only a short distance away. (Photo by author 2015).

18.

Fig.6 below; A violent storm - looking north to Poldhu (Photo by author March 2008)

Fig. 7 below; St. Mellanus Church and Tower, Mullion. (Photo by author 2015)

Strikingly and some may say shocking, it became apparent that, although only about 30 years of age, Buffani disclosed that this was his third total shipwreck. On each occasion he had been the sole survivor.

Buffani revealed to Harvey that the ship had broken up in no more than 20 minutes. At this point he was one of three sailors who had made their way to the bowsprit, where they held on until the section of the ship hit the cliffs. They were all thrown off, the other two being engulfed in a wave and thrown back into the sea where they were drowned (1).

The survivor Buffani managed to scale the cliff and grip onto the wet rock as the tide subsided and he was subsequently located by those searching for survivors.

The Vicar turned his attention to the name of the ship, but surprisingly, Buffani did not appear to know it.

The coast was littered with remains from the wreck and there was still the task of collecting what evidence was available in order to identify both the ship and the people who drowned in order that a Coroners Enquiry could be held.
A local policeman, Richard Barber, who lived in Mullion, had been informed of the wreck and by 4am, while it was still dark, he was on Poldhu beach only an hour or so after the disaster was reported.

20.

Amongst the remains of coffee and sugar there were three bodies, briefly described as follows;

 a) One of the females was a large woman, about 50 years of age, wearing no clothing at the time except two stockings, both on her left leg. She was eventually identified as a passenger from Batavia.

b) Another was aged about 23 years, with dark hair and finely formed features, but wearing drawers and stockings. She wore a gold clasp ring, and a gold heart shaped black enamelled locket with a photograph of a young man. She was eventually identified as Dutch and was apparently shortly to be married.

c) The third was the woman believed to be known to the Captain who had been confined a few weeks previously. The body of an infant was that of her child which when picked up wore a little night dress and cap and a coral necklace.

Sadly Coroners` inquests were regular affairs, held near to where the wrecks occurred and where the bodies could be stored. Many were not able to be identified and for health reasons alone needed to be disposed of as quickly and safely as possible.

Because thousands of ships and sailors from countries all around the world were to be found around the British coast, large coastal towns with ports had "consular" representation and interpreters were often called upon to translate reports of incidents involving shipwrecks. Information about the wreck was received by Mr Barrett, collector of Customs at Penzance, about 9am on the Tuesday morning. He sent an officer to take note of the wreck and any remains of the cargo which might come ashore. Also involved was John Matthews on behalf of Lloyds, Mr S. Higgs jnr, a consular official, and Mr Ludlow, the Netherlands vice-consul, to act for the owners.

A Bristol resident staying at Helston was informed of the sinking the following morning and decided to visit the scene with some friends. Afterwards he wrote an account of a visit to the scene of the wreck in the form of a letter which was published in the Bristol Mercury on 30th March 1867 (10).

Below is an extract from his letter,

Helston 26th March 1867,

"Sir- Intelligence having been brought here this Tuesday morning of the wreck of a large ship, I with three others drove down to the scene which we found to be situated at a small village called Mullion, about 5 miles down on the west coast of the Lizard. Here we found the coast literally strewn with fragments of the wreck and cane baskets for miles. The baskets which had contained coffee were to be seen by hundreds and as each one appears to be capable of containing four of five bushels

of the berries, the vessel must have been a very large one, and I think also a very old one as we were astonished to see the small fragments of old timber in which this vessel had broken up in so few hours. I think there was scarcely a vestige to be seen more than a yard in length except here and there part of a mast, but the greater part was in chips for firewood".

The writer then continues describing visiting Mullion Church, apparently having access to where the bodies were stored, and describes the scene in detail including the jewellery worn by the victims. There a lady had been put in charge of the supervision of the bodies. The letter continued,

"We next proceeded to the cottage of the coastguard man where we found the man who came ashore, as he told us, upon the bowsprit. He is a Greek seaman not more than 30 and who spoke enough English to provide us with some of the particulars. He said in evidence that there were 25 persons on board including three females, one of whom had given birth to a child, 20 days previously... is strange that the man that is saved cannot tell the name of the captain or that of the vessel, this is scarcely credible but that is the fact, his right arm is broken which he says was done 10 days ago, yet crippled as he was he is the only survivor of 25 persons, and he says this is the third time he has been a survivor from total wrecks. This unfortunate ship could be seen from this coast the greater part of Monday labouring and

making strenuous exertions to beat to windward to clear this fatal bay, but it came onto blow with thick weather from the south as night fell in and to most that know this horrid coast she was a doomed ship before morning unless a most unlikely change should take place in the night, but the gale lasted with great fury through the night, and this morning told the dreadful tale. To those unaccustomed to such scenes it seemed scarcely credible as we rode along the heights in the brilliant sunshine today, that there could have been such weather as to cause such a calamity only a few hours before".*

"P.S. The white coffee berries** line the sandy beach in such profusion as to be scarcely distinguishable from the white gravel found in these coves. The ship appears to have struck on a rugged point which divides two small coves and having struck exactly about mid-ships, broke off in the middle the forepart being washed up in fragments over the sunken rocks into one cove, and the stern into another."

Note;* It is often still the case that storms, heavy rain and strong winds occur overnight in this part of Cornwall. Low pressure systems often pass quickly and in the morning the winds have dropped leaving a bright, clear blue sky.

Note; **Java Coffee bushes grew on the alkaline slopes of active volcanoes. Without the alkaline soils the trees failed to produce berries. They were highly prized by Europeans for their quality.

The Coroner's Inquest

A Coroner's inquest was immediately called to ascertain the cause of the deaths and, the next day, Wednesday 27th March, Mr Rescorla, the County Coroner, held his inquest at the Old Inn at Mullion. (See Fig 5) Mr Nicholas, a local man, acted as the foreman of the Jury. The bodies of three ladies, a female infant, and a sailor lay nearby in Mullion Belfry (11).

They were all recognised as having been on board the Poldhu wreck. At that time no other bodies had been recovered from the cold winter sea. The only survivor, Georgio Buffani was examined by an interpreter Giacomo Carlo Balesteri of Penzance, and gave his evidence.

A most unfortunate situation had however occurred. At the time of the wreck two Dutch East Indiamen were at anchor at Falmouth, and the Captains heard of the loss and that the one survivor didn't know the name of the ship.

Requiring a positive identification, the two Dutch Captains came to Mullion to see Buffani and show to him the Official list of Dutch East Indiamen. Buffani picked out the *Kosmopoliet*-Captain Konig- and that is what he gave in his evidence, along with his record on the ship, the crew and the loss of three crewmen (2 dead, one sick) when they put into St. Helena.

First launched in 1854 in Dordrecht, the *Kosmopoliet* was a fast medium clipper built in the shipyard of Cornelis Grips, and worked the same route from Java to Rotterdam. She was well known for cutting the time taken from over 100 days to 74 days and was said to be the first Dutch Clipper, fully rigged with royals and sky sails on all 3 masts.

Buffani was aware of the cargo and details and could describe what happened. He said in evidence that the ship sailed from Batavia for Rotterdam on 25th November last. The crew consisted of 20 men all told, and there were 6 passengers, 3 ladies, 2 gentlemen and an English lad. On Saturday last they were off Falmouth, a port they could have entered, but did not. At 6am on Monday they were abreast of the Lizard in a SW to SSW wind. They then came under the land in Mounts Bay, and were tacking all day, unable to get out. When the vessel struck, everyone was on deck and the Captain cried bitterly. As previously reported, in 20 minutes the vessel broke up. He was on the jib boom with two other sailors and managed to save myself by jumping to the rocky cliff, the others were caught by the sea" (11).

The Coroner heard, how, on the Monday afternoon the Mousehole pilots observed the vessel trying to get off the eastern land, the Mullion Coast and about 4 pm was seen to "miss stays", more than once off Mullion Island, being unable to tack out of the Bay (9). She had no signal flying but it was thought that unless she was ably

manned she would have great difficulty in rounding the
Lizard (12). They decided not to go near her. After 8pm
the sky was clear but by 11pm it was blowing a
hurricane (8). Between 1am and 2am on the Tuesday
morning rockets were seen off Mullion from high ground
across the Mounts Bay near to Marazion, 10 miles (17
Km) away, but nothing was known of a wreck at Mullion
until after 3am (9).The likelihood was that the rockets
were not seen by the Coastguard at Mullion.

Police Constable Richard Barber, a resident of Mullion
told the court that he had gone to Poldhu Cove at about
4am, shortly after the wreck was reported. In evidence
he said that he found there the body of a woman
wearing only a pair of drawers and white stockings. She
also had two rings on the forefinger of her left hand, and
round her neck a gold locket and chain. The locket was
in the shape of a heart, one side coloured black, with 22
gold dots in it. The other side a Forget-me-not
embossed, with a photograph of a gentleman enclosed.
One of the rings was a plain gold wedding ring, the other
a foreign Keeper Ring.

 Buffani had identified this woman as a Dutch woman.
Shortly afterwards Constable Barber found a second
body of a woman, naked except for 2 stockings on one
foot. Buffani had identified her as an English lady. The
lady designated to look after the female bodies in the
Church Tower said that she was near her confinement.

A witness, F.W. West, identified a third woman as a French woman, with the initials "KL" on part of her clothes. There were four gold rings on the left hand, the first divided in two, on one part inside were the words "Sophie Willemin" and on the other part had "J Brugnot" engraved. The second ring had A.B. engraved on it, the third an embossed "Keeper" ring which could be opened. The fourth was a small green ring with 4 green stones and a pearl in the centre.

The jury returned their verdict in the case-

"Accidentally Drowned" (11)(14)(21).

This decision was far from the end of the matter. There still remained the issue of the identification of the ship, said by the survivor to be the *Kosmopoliet*. After the inquest jury had reached their verdict the Dutch Consul, Mr W Broad arrived. He was based at Falmouth and brought with him captains of 2 Dutch East Indiamen then anchored there. They asked if it was Captain Klaas Lammerts who had drowned, and when he was told it had been the *Kosmopoliet* which had been wrecked he said that this could not be true as that ship was not due for two weeks and questioned the verdict. Rev. Harvey however was now in possession of a piece of material found on the beach at Poldhu with a mark "6KL".

The Dutch skippers said at once that it must have been the *Jonkheer* which had gone aground, despite the Coroners' verdict.

On the Friday Mr Broad and the Dutch captains again visited Mullion and were handed a Masonic diploma found on the beach at Poldhu. Although saturated with sea water the name on it was clearly that of Klaas Lammerts. The Coroners' verdict had been wrongly recorded. It must have been the *Jonkheer Meester van de Wall van Putterschoek* on its homeward journey to Rotterdam from the East Indies, with its cargo valued at between £40- £50,000. Unfortunately nothing could be done now to change the verdict.

Work continued on the beaches to search for more property, no doubt now with assistance from many local people.

Ten more bodies were recovered after the 4th April. The bodies were in such a bruised and mutilated condition and no identification could be possible under any circumstances. On the finger of one of the bodies was a tiny gold ring, unlikely to have been worn by a working man and it was surmised that this may have been the body of one of the passengers.

The bodies were interred in Mullion Churchyard. The body of Sophia Woollett was laid to rest on 28th March 1867.

Records show that bodies believed to be those of Magen Utrecht and Willemin Sophie Brugnot and an unknown female plus two unknown males were also laid to rest there on the same day.

One body, described as that of an "unknown lad", was buried on the 5th April along with an unknown male and there were further burials on the 6th and 9th April (4).

Salvage of the "Treasure Chest"

Tons of coffee were collected from the beaches and carted to Penzance in the hopeful belief that they were capable of salvage and therefore could be auctioned. It was later reported that most of the coffee was unfit for use. Adverts were placed in local newspapers including the Western Daily Press (see below) advertising the sale of "... *superior java coffee more or less damaged*". Perhaps a clue to its state was in the advert which said that "... *a large portion being only slightly damaged*" and "*sold without reserve*".

> **FOR THE BENEFIT OF THE CONCERNED.**
>
> TO BE SOLD by AUCTION by Mr A. BERRYMAN, on WEDNESDAY, the 10th of April instant, at Noon, at the ALBERT STORES, near the Railway Station, PENZANCE,
>
> About 100 Tons of superior Java COFFEE more or less Damaged, salved from the clipper Ship Jonkheer Meester van de Wall van Puttershock, of Dordt, Capt. K. F. Lammerts, from Batavia for Rotterdam.
>
> This Coffee is well worthy the attention of Purchasers, a large portion being only slightly damaged, and will be Sold without reserve.
>
> For further particulars apply to ROBERT R. BROAD, Netherlands Vice-Consul, Falmouth; or to W. B. LUDLOW, Agent, Penzance.
>
> Dated Falmouth, April 4th, 1867.

Messrs. Jackson and Jones, of Penberth Cove were engaged to recover the sunken tin ballast from the seabed for a price of £15 per ton. It lay along with the anchors, chains and cables at a depth of 6 fathoms and during the salvage, equipment called Water Glasses and Tongs were used successfully to recover several tons of Ingots. Given the time of year and the usual colour of the sea in spring this was no mean feat. The total amount recovered is not reported. Under the direction of Mr W.B. Ludlow at Penzance, agent for the ship, 5 tons were recovered and brought to shore by mid May 1867.

When built, the ship's hull was bound with copper around the waterline, but none was reportedly found. During this salvage a small tin box about one foot square was recovered by Mr Jackson and the information was passed to Mr Nicholas to investigate this undoubted "treasure chest."

He called in Rev. Harvey to be present at the opening. Inside the slightly stained box were the personal treasures of the owner Sophia Woollett, her remains now lying in the village Churchyard.

The list of property recovered was as follows;

Two valid Bills of Exchange,
A bag with 119 x two and a half Guldens (Gold Coins),
A bag with 86 x Guldens (Gold Coins) (The 86 coins had been given to Mrs Sophia Woollett as change for a Bill at an Inn before she left Djakarta).
10x Ten Gulden Notes, 13 xTen Gulden Notes,1 Ten Gulden Note, 3x Ten Gulden notes, 3 x25 Gulden Notes, 1x25 Gulden Note, 1x 200 Gulden note (Java Bank), 1 x 40 Gulden note (Amsterdam Bank)
1x 7000 Gulden bill of exchange (Rotterdam Bank),
1x 40 Gulden note in the name of Rotterdam Bank,
3 Victoria Sovereigns,
5x small pieces of silver coin,
2 x gold bracelets,
2 x brooches,
3 x pr gold earrings, string of beads, locks of hair and the deceased own photograph by artists in Java.
A copy of the New Testament in English
A pocket book, for dance engagements.
A Will of Sophia Woollett (leaving all her property to her sister Charlotte Schroeder)

The Will was taken to Penzance where Mr Ludlow spent a great deal of time drying and forensically rearranging the pieces. Following publicity in the newspapers Rev. Harvey received a letter from Mrs Charlotte Schroeder of Nelson Street, Hulme, Manchester stating that her sister was one of the passengers on the *Jonkheer* and as a result the story of Sophia Woollett was revealed.

Sophia was 49 years of age and a widow. She had been in India for 20 years and had apparently lost her husband 9 years previously. She was now returning to England having accumulated a small fortune. Charlotte had received a letter posted in January from the island of St. Helena, in the middle of the south Atlantic Ocean, to her home in Manchester explaining that Sophia would be returning very soon with the *Jonkheer*.

Her body had been recovered after the wreck and it had been thought that she was the Dutch lady, but in fact she was born in Holland of English parents. When found, her nightdress was marked SW and this and other linen which had since come ashore had been accurately described in Mrs Schroeder's letter, enough to assist the police in an accurate identification.

There was another twist to the tale. Further to the stories which appeared in the newspapers another claimant appeared in the shape of the husband of Sophia Woollett. There was also a letter from a Rotterdam solicitor, Mr Cooke, informing the consul that Mrs Woollett had her personal life savings with her when she made the journey. The husband had supposedly gone missing or had died 9 years earlier. It appeared from his story that he had separated from her before she went abroad, and had then mysteriously disappeared.

For locating the box and contents the salvors received ⅓ of the property value, Mrs Schroeder and Cooke received ⅔, but not before the payment of legal expenses had taken their share, leaving little of value. For many years after the wreck of the *Jonkheer* coffee bags were laid down on local cottage floors as mats. Cane and bamboo sugar baskets, split and fastened with stakes and were used to protect gardens from the strong scouring coastal winds (26)(27).

Life is not short of surprises. Rev. Harvey wrote that the widow of Captain Klaas Lammerts lived in Rue de Plank, Dordrecht and she wrote offering a £5 reward for recovery of her husband's body - but it was never identified among those recovered (1,p73). Records in Holland indicate that in April 1852 he married Margareta van de Plank who was born in 1828 in Dordrecht and they lived in Groenmarkt. They had three children born in 1853, 1856 and 1857 (33).

For Rev. Harvey there was an unanswered question which he took with him to his grave. He was apparently greatly affected by the wreck and wrote letters to the press about the urgent need for a local Lifeboat and a better system of dealing with rescues. On the night of the wreck the Coastguard reported that about 3am he had seen a large vessel in danger. That was when the tide had ebbed for four hours. When villagers went down to the coast they apparently found coffee and parts of the wreck lying right up at high water (1,p73).That, to Harvey, left an important unanswered question. The vessel must, therefore, he suggested, have struck some time before or about the time of high water, and not later. Were the sounds of voices heard by the Rev. Harvey at high tide the previous evening, disturbing his reading, the last cries of drowning people as the vessel was breaking up? Harvey recorded that the following morning he was roused early and informed of the wreck, before visiting Buffani about 9am (1,p 69 &73).

 What can now be revealed is that on the evening of Monday 25th March 1867 high tide was in fact not at 11pm but between 8pm and 8.30pm. The tide had, in fact, been receding by two and a half hours when he heard, or fancied he heard the sounds of many voices. Perhaps, the "voices" were indeed a premonition of an impending disaster or fears still raw from the many January storms and wrecks. The next high tide was between 8.19 am and 8.46am the following morning (1)(7) (7a). See appendix for High Water Times March 1867, Falmouth & Penzance)

Record in the Lloyds Register 1884

The Lloyds Agency List was a record of wrecks and casualties to ships on the coasts west of the Lizard including Mounts Bay and Lands End to the Gurnards Head, being the extent of the Lloyds agency port of Penzance. Compiled by WD Mathews and sons, Lloyds

Agents Penzance and published in local newspapers. There were 22 entries for 1867.The fifteenth entry for the year was on March 26th, that of the *Jonkheer Meester van de Wall van Putterschoek*, 650 tons, lost at Mullion Cliffs, carrying a general cargo. The ship was a total loss, ship and cargo very valuable, loss of several passengers, estimated loss £40-50,000. 24 lives were reported lost; one man was saved from the rocks (28).

A letter was received by the editor of the Western Morning News from E.G. Harvey, written on March 30th 1867. The letter below shows the frustration that people felt at the loss of life and property involving shipwrecks at this period of Cornish history brought about by increasing storm activity and flooding.

"Sir- upwards of 50 human lives have been lost during the past three months, through lack of a secure anchorage in Mounts Bay for embayed or distressed vessels.
Property in ships and cargoes to the amount of many thousands has also been sacrificed from the same cause, and in the same short time. Now an expenditure of £15,000 would I am credibly informed, render the Cove at Mullyon a safe harbourage at all states of tide for 20-30 vessels. If this be so, and still no provision be made against awful shipwrecks as have occurred in Mounts Bay this winter, there surely will be great short sightedness, to say the least of it, somewhere E.G. Harvey.

The first Mullion Lifeboat, "*Daniel J Draper*" was brought by train to Penzance from London on 10th September 1867 and launched with great ceremony. The new crew rowed her across the Mounts Bay to Mullion Cove on 13th September, where she began her role. Just over a month later on October 21st at her first call out the crew were recorded as saving 4 lives from the barque *Achilles* wrecked at Polurrian in a rescue involving the coastguard and rocket apparatus which saved a further 14 of the crew (3). There were two other Lifeboats (*Edith* and *Nancy Newbon*) stationed here before the Station eventually closed in July 1908 after 33 Launches in 40 years (3).

World trade expanded, with thousands of steam ships replacing the more vulnerable sailing ships of the mid 1800s, but it was improvements in weather forecasting, wireless telegraphy, and later radio communication which offered the greatest improvement in protection for ships and sailors.
Coincidentally, thanks to Guglielmo Marconi and his colleagues, many important experiments and developments in radio communication took place in 1901 in a field adjacent to the SW Coastal Path, on a headland on the south side of Poldhu, only a few metres away from where the remains of the *Jonkheer* lie with no commemoration for the lives lost. The storms and shipwrecks of 1867 have largely been forgotten, but they provide a tantalising glimpse into world maritime,

and local Cornish history. The *Jonkheer* was one of hundreds of ships wrecked in Cornish waters, but one which left an indelible mark on the lives of many people. The Captain and crew were experienced, yet no doubt keen to reach Rotterdam after being away from home so long away. Did the earlier loss of 3 crew members make the ship difficult to sail or were there other reasons? Why did the captain apparently decide not to seek help from shore until it was too late? Did the large cargo of tin ballast affect the way the ship was handling in the storm?

The available evidence suggests that the storm increased in intensity later on the Monday and into the black night. The depleted crew would likely have been exhausted trying to tack all day and into the night.

Captain Klaas Lammerts was left with no alternative but to hope that the ship could weather the storm and reach land at a safer spot, perhaps on the sandy beach at Poldhu Cove but men, women, and a young baby sadly all died that night in terrible circumstances- all except one man Georgio Buffani who was spared to tell his story. The wreck of the *Jonkheer Meester van de Wall van Putterschoek,* and the loss of so many lives, was a tragedy recognised in newspapers of the day as *"The most disastrous wreck of the year"* (30).

The final word comes by way of a quotation from the
Royal Cornwall Gazette of November 30th 1872 (2)(31).

*"From Falmouth to Lands End there is no shelter but a
roadstead in S or SW gales. Mounts Bay is but a man-
trap when the wind is from that quarter, and if a
foreigner without a pilot could find Mullion Roads in a
night as black as a pocket he must have uncommonly
good anchors to trust for a safe lodging. There is
something tragic in the thought that to a ship travelling
helplessly down upon a lee shore in the darkness of the
night or in a fog or in one of those storms which
confounded the sky, and the sea in one abyss of cloud,
the lights that twinkle from habitable homes are no
better than the wandering fires that beguile a lost
traveller on a morass."*

Appendix 1 Ship History- In May 1855 the keel of a ship was laid at ship makers Cornelis Gips and sons of Dordrecht in South Holland under the direction of Mr J van Wageningen. The ship was to be called Jonkheer van de Wall van Putterschoek (Dordrecht Courant 10.5.1855) The ship was readied for launch from their wharf at Merwede on 16th August 1856.(Dordrecht Courant 15.8.1856) The following day under the direction of the prospective Captain Klaas Folkert Lammerts she was launched. Although not far from the sea, Rotterdam was the official start of the journey. However the flooding and reflooding of the rivers changed the landscape repeatedly created new river channels on the flat flood plains. The journey actually began from Hellevoetsluis or Brouwershaven, 20 km south of Rotterdam.

The Jonkheer was recorded as being 41metres 16cm (135 foot) in length, 9metres 76cm (32 foot) in width and depth 6metres 51cms (21 foot in depth). She weighed 651 tons. In the copy of the original ships drawings the lay- out of the three masts can be seen. The main cargo storage was in the front three quarters of the ship with cabins and passenger facilities to the stern. Below see copies of original plans for the Jonkheer. (Courtesy Jean van Wageningen)

 Banka or Bangka Island lies in the Java sea off the east coast of Sumatra. In 1812 the Sultan of Palembang ceded the rights to Britain and in 1814 Britain transferred them to the Dutch in exchange for the rights to the spice trading centre of Cochin in India. Tin ore was so plentiful at "Bangka" that in 1813 alone over 2000 tons was raised by the Chinese miners, equal to about half the annual production of Cornwall.

Appendix 2. Table of estimated distance in Nautical Miles (nm.) covered by the Jonkheer on the journey from Rotterdam to Jakarta and also by return via St.Helena.

Outward Journey-Rotterdam to Buenos Aires 6000 nm.- Buenos Aires to Cape of Good Hope 4000 nm-Cape of Good Hope to SW Australia 4500 nm.- SW Australia to (Batavia) Jakarta 2250 nm.

Inward Journey- (Batavia) Jakarta – Cape of Good Hope 7250 nm., Cape of Good Hope to St. Helena- 1800 nm., St. Helena to Cornwall 4000 nm.* (wrecked), Cornwall to Rotterdam 460 nm.

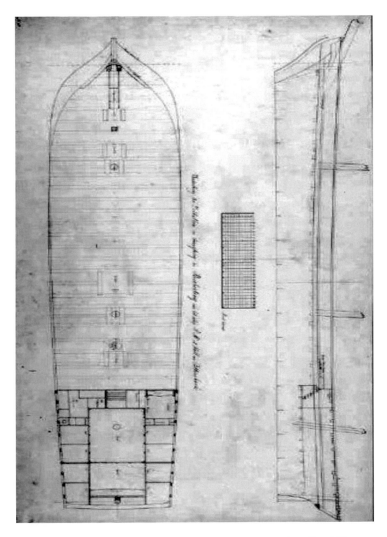

<u>Appendix 3</u> Copy of Plans used to construct the "Jonkheer". Hull and Mast arrangement below.

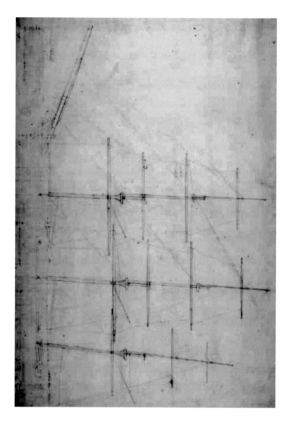

Appendix 4 Below; High Water Tide Table –Falmouth and Penzance 22 March-27 March 1867 (See Page 35) (7a)

TIDE TABLE.—TIME OF HIGH WATER.

		Falmouth.		Penzance & St. Ives	
		MORN. h. m.	AFT. h. m.	MORN. h. m.	AFT h. m
Friday, March...	22 ...	6 30 ...	6 48 ...	6 3 ...	6 21
Saturday..........	23 ...	7 5 ...	7 23 ...	6 18 ...	6 56
Sunday.............	24 ...	7 40 ...	7 57 ...	7 13 ...	7 30
Monday	25 ...	8 13 ...	8 30 ...	7 46 ...	8 3
Tuesday.	26 ...	8 46 ...	9 3 ...	8 19 ...	8 36
Wednesday.......	27 ...	9 23 ...	9 42 ...	8 56 ...	9 15

References include,

1. Mullyon, Its history scenery and antiquities. 1875. E.G. Harvey B.A Vicar
2. Cornish Shipwrecks; The South Coast. Larn and Carter 1969, 7153 4289 4
3.A history of Mullion Cove Cornwall.R. Felce, 2012 ISBN 978-0-9569895-1-2
4. http://www.genuki.org.uk/big/eng/Cornwall/Mullion/#ChurchRecords
5. blockland.dordtenazoeker.nl
6. Google Earth
6a An economic history of Indonesia 1800-2010 van Zaanden, Marks.
6b "The War for all the Oceans..." Roy and Lesley Adkins. 2006.
7. Royal Cornwall Gazette (RCG) 21.3.1867
7a RCG 21.3.1867
8. RCG 28.3.1867
9. Western Times 29.3.1867
10. Bristol Mercury 30.3.1867
11. Lakes Falmouth Packet and Cornwall Advertiser 30.3.1867
12. Westmoreland Gazette 30.3.1867
13.Waterford Mail 3.4.1867
14. Louth and N. Lincs Advertiser 6.4.1867
15. Paisley Herald and Renfrewshire Advertiser 6.4.1867
16. Whitstable Times and Herne Bay Herald 6.4.1867
17. Western Times 8.4.1867
18. Western Daily Press 9.4.1867
19. London Standard 16.4.1867
20. South Shields Gazette 17.4.1867
21. RCG 18.4.1867
22. South London Press 20.4.1867
23. RCG 24.1.1867
24. RCG 16.5.1867
25. South Shields Gazette 20.5.1867
26. Hereford Times 1.6.1867
27. Illustrated Police News 1.6.1867
28. Cornishman 26.6.1884
29.Western Times 11.9.1867
30. RCG 2.1.1868
31. RCG 30.11.1872
32. e- mail J. van Wangenigen 27.7.15
33. e-mail (partenrederij) J van Wangeningen 28.7.15